BRIGHT NOTES

FRANNY AND ZOOEY AND NINE STORIES BY J.D. SALINGER

D1523956

Intelligent Education

INFLUENCE PUBLISHERS

Nashville, Tennessee

BRIGHT NOTES: Franny and Zooey and Nine Stories

www.BrightNotes.com

ISBN: 978-1-645422-58-7 (Paperback)

ISBN: 978-1-645422-59-4 (eBook)

Published in accordance with the U.S. Copyright Office Orphan Works and Mass Digitization report of the register of copyrights, June 2015.

Originally published by Monarch Press.

Charlotte A. Alexander, 1966

2020 Edition published by Influence Publishers.

Interior design by Lapiz Digital Services. Cover Design by Thinkpen Designs.

Printed in the United States of America.

Library of Congress Cataloging-in-Publication Data forthcoming.

Names: Intelligent Education

Title: BRIGHT NOTES: Franny and Zooey and Nine Stories

Subject: STU004000 STUDY AIDS / Book Notes

CONTENTS

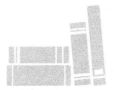

INTRODUCTION TO J. D. SALINGER

....

J. D. Salinger (Jerome David Salinger) was born in New York City in 1919 to Sol and Miriam Jillich Salinger (his father was Jewish; his mother, Scotch Irish). He has a sister Doris 8 years his senior. He attended public schools on Manhattan's upper West Side, the private McBurney School in Manhattan, and then Valley Forge Military Academy in Pennsylvania, from which he graduated in 1936. His college experience was brief: a summer session at New York University, a short-story writing class at Columbia University taught by Whit Burnett, co-editor of Story, and a short period at Ursinus College in Pennsylvania.

Uninterested in joining his father's meat importing business, he was writing fiction at least by the time he was twenty (his first published story is dated 1940). Of further biographical note is his military service during World War II, including counter-intelligence training in Devonshire, England (the setting for part of "For Esme-with Love and Squalor"); he also participated in D-Day beach landings and European campaigns. During the post-war period he has lived, in addition to New York, in Tarry-town, N.Y.; Westport, Conn. and Cornish, N.H.

In 1955 he married Claire Douglas; they have a daughter and a son.

Salinger is noted for what has been called a "reverse exhibitionism," that is, a determination to keep his life private. If he is a recluse, however it seems to have become so by a more gradual process than is usually pointed out (he was, after all, in this teen years, an active student at Valley Forge prep school, participating in several clubs, the dramatic organization, and in the preparation of the academy yearbook as literary editor). Withdrawal may have been the result of disenchantment perhaps with the irritant, nuisance element success can bring, as well as a general seeking after a peaceful existence which was not uncommon to young men who survived the grim years of actual involvement in World War II. In 1950, for example, he was not above visiting (while living at Tarrytown, N. Y.) a short-story class at Sarah Lawrence College, although he remarked afterwards, "I enjoyed the day, but it isn't something I'd ever want to do again." Since then he has turned down invitations for public appearances (such as participation in the various writers' conferences which are run regularly in the United States and abroad).

In Cornish, N. H., where he has lived since the fervor of publicity over *The Catcher in the Rye*, he seems to have stressed in "nuisance values" of success, by putting a high fence around his house. Since this is the case, it seems a wise policy to follow the lead of one of Salinger's more scrupulous critics (Warren French) who admits in the preface to his book about the author (J. D. Salinger): "I bear no news about Salinger himself-I would consider it impertinent to invade his cherished privacy."

BACKGROUND AND PUBLICATION OF NINE STORIES

By 1941, when he was 22, Salinger was publishing in well-paying magazines such as Collier's and Esquire, and he continued to write during World War II. But it was in 1948 that he began to find real recognition, with the publication of three stories which later were to appear in the collection, *Nine Stories:* "A Perfect Day for Bananafish," "Uncle Wiggily in Connecticut," and "Just Before the War with the Eskimos," all appearing in the New Yorker, certainly a prestigious sign. In 1949 and 1950 three more stories from his collection were published - "The Laughing Man," "Down at the Dinghy," and "For Esme -with Love and Squalor." The collection itself, of course, was not issued until 1953, since when it has enjoyed lasting popularity without ever reaching the top-selling levels. (The story "Uncle Wiggily in Connecticut," titled *My Foolish Heart,* was turned into a movie by Samuel Goldwyn studios with Susan Hayward and Dana Andrews. It was a distorted version which Salinger disapproved of highly, a factor which has probably contributed to urge his continuing refusal to allow further screen or television productions of his writings.)

BACKGROUND AND PUBLICATION OF CATCHER IN THE RYE

In the late '40s and early '50s, while the pieces from *Nine Stories* were being published separately, Salinger was undoubtedly trying to work into a novel his earlier stories about Holden Caulfield. (In 1946, for instance, a novelette about Holden had been accepted for publication, then was withdrawn by Salinger). *The Catcher in the Rye* became upon publication in 1951 what might be termed an almost-immediate success. As a midsummer Book-of-the-Month Club selection, for example, it certainly exposed Salinger to a larger audience than he had hitherto enjoyed-if, indeed, "enjoyed" is the proper word, since the degree of popularity was enough to disturb Salinger, who directed that a large photograph of his face be removed from the third and subsequent issuings of the book. He remarked later to a friend that "I feel tremendously relieved that the season for success for *The Catcher in the Rye* is nearly over. I enjoyed a small part of it, but most of it I found hectic and professionally and personally demoralizing." Reviews of the novel were mixed, from out-and-out approval to questions about Salinger's attitudes, the colloquial style, the focus on an adolescent boy, and, of course, the issue which has since attracted attention-whether the book was fit for young readers. Thus *The Catcher in the Rye*, especially since issuance as a paperback in 1953, has been, curiously, both stipulated for and banned from high school and college reading lists (the foundation for, or lack of foundation for, such controversy is explored in the following pages of detailed analysis of the novel).

LIST OF SALINGER'S WORKS

The Catcher in the Rye, 1951; *Nine Stories,* 1953; *Franny and Zooey,* 1961; *Raise High the Roof Beam, Carpenters and Seymour: An Introduction,* 1963. (As indicated above, all subsequent works listed after *The Catcher in the Rye* are short stories, most of them published prior to collective issuance.)

A BRIEF LOOK AT SALINGER'S THEMES AND ATTITUDES

Following are some of the issues pertinent to any detailed analysis of Salinger's work, issues which are treated in the "Comments" below as well as in the short summary of what Salinger's critics have had to say about his writings: (a) His **protagonists** are often intelligent, sensitive, and very aware adolescents, or adults who, in either case, seek their own identity in relation to an external world with which they find themselves more or less at variance. (b) Alienation or disenchantment with the so-called "adult" world figures largely in Salinger's writings, often emphasized by rather "average" characters (parents, teachers, marriage partners, etc.) who interrelate with the troubled **protagonist**. (c) A definition of the "adult" world is sometimes sought or offered-it may be viewed as commercialized, materialistic, phony, ugly, grotesque-all suggestive of reasons for the sensitive **protagonist** to retreat from it, in reality or symbolically (for example, through madness, or suicide, or simply by introversion and fantasy). (d) Salinger is very concerned with the rather ancient question of innocence and experience in human lives, and how the life experience which is inevitable may best be realized instrue spiritual growth, instead of producing, say, a tough cynicism (such as that of Eloise in "Uncle Wiggily in Connecticut," or of young Selena and Eric in "Before the War with the Eskimos"). (e) Sometimes true "love" of humanity seems to be the solution offered, as in "Teddy". (f) Salinger's style includes a rather inspired use of detail - he can characterize in an instant's phrase - and a good deal of 20th-century slang, vocabulary of adolescents, colloquialisms.

NINE STORIES

....

"A PERFECT DAY FOR BANANAFISH"

This introductory story of the collection treats the now famous Glass and Carpenter families of *Franny and Zooey,* and *Raise High the Roof Beam, Carpenters and Seymour: an Introduction.* The extremely precocious and sensitive children of the Glass family include Seymour (featured in this story); Buddy (a writer); Boo Boo (featured in "Down at the Dinghy" in this collection); the twins, Walt and Waker (Walt is deceased, Waker is a Roman Catholic priest); Zooey, an actor, and Franny, a college student (featured in *Franny and Zooey*). Mr. Glass is Jewish, his wife, Irish. The family represents urban, upper-middle-class Jewish society. There are suggestions that the Glass family is a kind of Yoknapatawpha County (created by William Faulkner) located on Park Avenue, New York City.

Is It A "Slick" Story?

This story is a cool, suspenseful one. Some critics view "A Perfect Day for Bananafish" as "slick," a charge sometimes directed at Salinger for his so-called "New Yorker type" of stories. It is, instead, carefully constructed to build suspense, withholding the **climax** until the final line. Between the first and last sentences, too, information is cleverly accumulated so as to leave the reader in doubt about what is happening, who is sane, who is less than sane.

Other critics hold that the story is told with subtle suggestiveness, a highly symbolic, often ambiguous work. Salinger manages to suggest a great personal agony through symbolism, a symbolism that foreshadows the story's startling ending.

Symbolism

Seymour Glass's fantasy about bananafish directly reflects his alienation from the adult world. The tragic bananafish suggest children of rare sensitivity and intellectual gifts who are unable to cope with the hostile and cruel world which they grow up in. They are forced to submit to and take part in the hostile, savage battle of life (to lose their innocence). Caught in the trap, they cannot extricate themselves and they die (of "banana fever"), swallowed up by a world which is virtually unbearable to them.

The implication is that Seymour was such a child; his capacity for pain (particularly in a self-destructive, unsuitable marriage) has turned into an agony which he can no longer bear. In addition, Seymour seems horrified to think that the little girl has glimpsed the fate that is in store for her. (Some critics, however, have suggested that Sybil glimpsed death, implying perhaps a suggestion of murder.)

Alienation

Seymour is totally alienated from the adult world to the point of even concealing his body from it, as in the elevator scene which suggests Seymour's distaste at being exposed to adult scrutiny.

Seymour relaxes with the child. He is able to communicate with the unspoiled, spontaneous world of children; he can afford to be himself; that is, unclothed and transparent, as the child's mispronunciation of his name suggests. Seymour's dialogue is eccentric; it can be fitted into the child's world as well as a lunatic's world. It is, however, appropriate to a child's imagination-full of shiftings from topic to topic, abrupt non sequiturs, teasing, etc.

It is obvious to the reader that Seymour is very fond of children. With Sybil he feels less alienated; he is able to make himself vulnerable in a close relationship without feelings of insecurity. The child's responses are honest responses that Seymour can always count on, not the out-growth of adult conditioning. In the elevator scene, we are aware that the woman was unwilling, and probably unable, to be honest and admit the truth to Seymour.

It is difficult to tell how much of a misfit Seymour is in his world, because those who view him from the outside suggest that his behavior is antisocial, even perhaps mad. Yet that behavior is never clearly specified. The suggestions that are made are inconclusive, hardly convincing the reader that the young man is psychotic.

When we fit these details into the context of Seymour's conduct and conversation with little Sybil, we wonder if they can be looked upon as the gestures of a person who looks at life (or would like to look at life) more through the eyes of a child than of an adult. This explanation would explain his associational, absurd conversation with Sybil and his sense of humor, which is hard to place. At any rate, Seymour seems genuinely to understand and like children-he certainly knows how to entertain Sybil. He is benevolent and playful, not hostile.

The **theme** of alienation of children from parents is suggested in the brief interchange between Sybil and her mother. They speak to one another, but there is no meaningful communication between them at all.

Muriel Glass

We begin to ask what sort of woman Muriel Glass is as we observe her behavior. From the accumulation of details emerges a figure who seems quite content to occupy herself with herself, and who is capable of showing interest in others only in a very detached manner. Her chatter is superficial, her concerns, shallow. She is coolly indifferent toward life, her husband and his illness. Her primary concern is her physical appearance. She does not share her mother's anxious concern.

Muriel seems to refuse to regard Seymour as very ill and considers it sufficient that there is a psychiatrist nearby who will be on hand to take care of him, if necessary. Otherwise, Muriel seems inclined to leave Seymour to his own devices. This story illustrates one of Salinger's favorite **themes** - the alienation of the individual. Sybil and her mother are not capable of communicating; Muriel and Seymour are worlds apart.

"UNCLE WIGGILY IN CONNECTICUT"

Painful Reality

This story once again enables Salinger to explore human situations in terms of loss of innocence, conflicts between fantasy and reality, the gradual acquisition of painful experience which often marks the passing of youth. The lives of the two main characters are gradually revealed to be bleak and purposeless. At the end of the story, however, Eloise seems vaguely aware of her troubled lack of adjustment to the realities of her life.

The Nostalgic Past

Eloise is a woman of troubled identity. She resists the present-her roles as wife and mother-preferring to view herself as a girl of 18 or 19, who was happily in love and who needed to have fun, to laugh at life. We get the impression that Eloise remembers nostalgically only the good times and the humorous incidents of her past life with Walt, apparently her first love. He has taken on a kind of exaggerated, dreamlike stature in her imagination. (Walt is one of the Glass twins mentioned earlier.)

Eloise romanticizes the past, looking to it for humor, warmth, security, sympathy and love. Eloise's lost, cherished dream represents her adolescent rebellion against the demands of psychological and emotional maturity. She appears to feel that she has missed something or has been cheated of something. Her discontent is built-in (self-made); unless she accepts the reality of the present, no one can make her feel less alienated from life and people. By resisting responsibility, Eloise reveals that the only thing she has been cheated of are her desires-particularly the desire to avoid facing reality and the meaning of her own actions.

Eloise's Present Life

Eloise has a very cynical view of her marriage; her pleasant past is always more appealing, by comparison, than her husband. Her marriage is without trust, warmth or love. Eloise seems afraid that Lew will spoil what she treasures so dearly about the past. But since, so far as the reader can see, Lew is certainly not an unperceptive boor, we must conclude that Eloise is unconsciously afraid that her dream world will disintegrate, that telling Lew would somehow admit the light of day, the air of reality, and that she might have to take a close look at herself and her real life.

As is often the case with Salinger, Lew is one of those characters the reader must picture without his actually appearing, by piecing together his personality from remarks of other characters, however exaggerated or curious. (Through such characters Salinger indicates the complexity of real life, where people exhibit many faces to the world, and our judgment about them must be made from a gathering of abundant and diverse observations.) Eloise considers him lacking in youth, intelligence and sensitivity. From the evidence presented, however, the reader concludes that he is probably an average man, fairly hardworking and the object of strong hostility from his wife.

Childhood Fantasy

Ramona emerges as a pathetic child, so lonely and isolated that she has been forced to invent a fantasy life. Ramona feels safer with her imaginary companion than with the real people she knows. She protects herself from pain by being secretive and withdrawn, by refusing to show affection, by behaving stubbornly. In the final scene, her tears are those of a lost, lonely child who wants and needs warmth and love.

Eloise is at a loss to understand Ramona and does not choose to take the responsibility too seriously. They are completely isolated from one another. Salinger presents their lack of communication brilliantly in dialogue. Eloise understands her daughter no better than she feels her husband would understand her secret. (Eloise is really an alienated stranger in her own house, alienated from both her husband and her daughter.)

Given Ramona's bleak environment, devoid of emotional ties, her treatment of her "companion" is not entirely unanticipated. It may be interpreted in two ways. Either she is repressed to the point where she is almost unable to be close to any other person, real or imaginary. Or, Ramona may realize the harshness of the world around her, and she therefore decides to arm herself against it by initiating the loss of Jimmy before he can be taken away from her. Like a child, however, she quite naturally invents a replacement instantly.

Adult Fantasy

Just as Ramona has a defense mechanism against the hostile world, so her mother preserves the illusions of the past. Neither of them has fully joined the real world. But Eloise preserves her illusions, not only as a defense, but as an escape - an escape from a life that is adult and therefore demands more than shallow social activities and childish jokes. (Notice that Eloise's jokes throughout the story have a grammar-school quality; they lack subtlety.) The child's fantasy is much more sympathetic, precisely because she is a child and therefore unable to cope with or understand the hostility around her.

Eloise's fantasy life surrounds Walt, of whom the reader gets two opposite impressions. One must decide whether he is really humorous and nice, or whether he is just the wisecracker that Eloise insists her husband views him as. To Eloise, of course, he represents youth, which she tends to glorify. The reader suspects that Walt might not have had the qualities of endurance needed for adult responsibilities, just as Eloise does not.

Eloise's fantasy life has had a devastating effect on her, leaving her a sterile person with a distorted set of values. She is unmoved by the events and people that surround her in her daily life. She needs Mary Jane desperately for two reasons, neither of which is flattering to Mary Jane: as a sounding board to relieve her loneliness and as a figure from the past who can help her relive it. Considering her present sterility, Salinger's comment about her fertility is extremely effective, by way of contrast.

In the bedroom scene, Ramona's and Eloise's fantasy lives clash. Eloise tries to destroy her daughter's fantasy world. Eloise's motivation for this action is presented ambiguously. She may be hoping to save Ramona the later feelings of loss and discontent which she herself now experiences. Or her action may have been a mixture of both compassion and cruelty. The latter is more likely to be the case, since there is a strong suggestion that Ramona is Walt's child, in which case Ramona is a constant reminder of Walt - a reminder that Eloise, subconsciously, probably wants both to preserve and to destroy.

The symbolism surrounding Ramona's glasses is also ambiguous. Salinger makes a point of describing the placement of Ramona's glasses in the bedroom scene. The author's intent is not clear; the gesture may be symbolic of finality - the past is indeed dead. Or it may suggest that Eloise wants Ramona to "see" well, perhaps better than her mother has been able to.

Facing Reality

Throughout the story, Mary Jane has been asking sensible questions in an attempt to get Eloise to look at her husband and at life a little more realistically, a little less hypercritically. Though not a happy person, Mary Jane seems to comprehend the real world more clearly than Eloise does, to be more capable of dealing with it. She seems genuinely interested in Ramona. However, Mary Jane, too, suffers from a deep-seated loneliness, and Salinger intends her to represent a product of the chaotic years of World War II-translated into terms of affluent Eastern suburbia or of career-conscious New York City.

The central question in the interpretation of Eloise's character is whether the bedroom scene indicates a minor step in the direction of reality. Considering the final sentences of the story, however, one has to conclude that it does not. The desperation in Eloise's voice is tinged with tragedy. She needs reassurance, but a reassurance that the reader is aware no one can give her. The futility of her yearning for the past will be interpreted by the reader as a tragedy or a betrayal, according to his view of the meaning of Eloise's evasion of reality.

Literary Technique

This story is one of the most successful in the volume. It is told with great economy in a compressed style. Salinger captures the bleakness of the scene in carefully drawn dialogue that reveals the essence of the characters. The selection of each event is deliberately calculated to reveal character indirectly; the story has no irrelevancies. The "Uncle Wiggily" device to reveal the true identity of Ramona's father is indirect, but a brilliant example of Salinger's artistry.

"JUST BEFORE THE WAR WITH THE ESKIMOS"

This story deals with the comfortable, bourgeois, New York society of lonesome rich children. It displays what one critic has called the "wounded affections" of the "upper-class orphan." Salinger is describing here the causes and origins of the loss of innocence.

Chaotic, Disordered Lives

By accumulating significant details, Salinger sketches the life of the Selenas, the Franklins and the Erics of the world, as seen by Ginnie Mannox. Theirs is a disorganized and joyless world. They live disordered lives among disordered, tasteless furnishings. Symbolic of this disorder is Selena's brother Franklin-childishly unable to control his emotions, reacting inappropriately to his hurt finger, perhaps a symbol for all the pain of his life.

The appearance of Eric increases the sensation of a world askew. Eric's responses, like Franklin's, are exaggerated. He frets nervously about insignificant things, revealing deeper personal problems and psychological disorder. Eric, although he has a peculiar kind of childlike innocence, is one of Salinger's misfits, who seem lost and at variance with the world of their parents, who are quite often absent.

In sum, the household presented here is hectic and loveless, one in which the children are isolated, neglected and left to their own devices. Each has found a method of coping with his own pain: Franklin, in emotionality and cursing; Eric, in homosexuality; and Selena, in undertones of hostility. Franklin's attacks on Ginnie's sister reveal a defensive hostility used to cover his disappointment at her lack of response. The pathetic offer of the sandwich reveals Franklin's only way of making a gesture of friendship; he is emotionally frozen.

Aimlessness

In this brief story, Salinger captures one of the most prevalent symptoms of many post-World War II adolescents (particularly of the upper-middle-class) - the somewhat chronic feelings of alienation and purposelessness. Many children in this environment are the product of a destructive blend of pampering and neglect, a blend which Salinger seems to understand well and is able to portray convincingly.

Franklin, for example, seems neither like a boy nor a man- he is unfinished, incomplete, as wandering and lost as the disordered world from which he emerges. That he cannot (and we assume, chronically cannot) be on time for appointments suggests that discipline is nonexistent in his life. The reader imagines him going the rounds of purportedly aesthetic adventures with his similarly purposeless friend Eric. His values seem shallow, and what things he does value he doesn't seem to exert much effort to achieve. He lacks direction, lacks a career, lacks a profound view of life and his place in it.

Eric is a lost person, too. (It is suggested that the lack of close family ties and the general chaos of the World War II years have contributed to making these young men drifters.) Eric is unable to cope with a world devoid of warmth and security, and has sought love and affection in homosexual relationships. But he is even a loser here, too, since his offers of affection have been rejected. He covers up his pain by a generous quantity of self-pity and snobbery. He and Franklin are opposites in many ways, thus complementing each other.

Selena emerges, not as an individualized portrait, but as an almost abstract, inevitable product of her environment. She is apparently as disorganized and irresponsible as her brother, and she is probably often given to lying as a protection against the outside world (the reader doubts that her mother is really ill). At the same time, Selana seems eager for attention and friendship.

Ginnie Mannox

Ginnie seems to be one of Salinger's sensitive, observant and compassionate protagonists. At any rate, she reaches a new awareness as the story develops. Her anger dissolves as she gains insight into Selena's life. Gradually, the anger is replaced by sympathy for the empty life she finds in the Graff household.

Ginnie is practical and unsentimental, like so many young people in Salinger's stories. Yet she is capable of sympathy and understanding, and of revising judgments when that is in order. We see this in her absorption in the details of the Graff family and the resulting compassion that prompts her to offer friendship to Selena.

Ginnie sees Selena and Franklin (and perhaps even Eric) as innocent, childlike, defenseless in an adult world that seems indifferent to them. They are as defenseless, in fact, as the baby chick who certainly needed warmth and attention to survive and grow.

Significance of the Eskimos

Franklin attacks the concept of war and the draft, but one senses that envy lies very close to the surface veneer of hostility. He seems to feel that the men who volunteer to go to war are at least fulfilling some chosen purpose; he is bitter that others fought while he was resigned to a post in a factory.

"THE LAUGHING MAN"

This story has a dual text, a fantastical account of "The Laughing Man" serial which parallels the relationship between John and Mary, as seen through the eyes of a nine-year-old narrator. At the end of the story, the "dual" romances collapse simultaneously, with an acute impact of tragedy upon the boys.

Significance of "The Laughing Man"

No symbol in Salinger's writing could more chillingly evoke the **theme** of loneliness, alienation and isolation, than that of the Laughing Man. He is the ultimate misfit: a grotesque, disfigured man whose disfigurement is partially the result of a decision of his parents. In spite of this, however, he triumphs over the hostile world and overcomes his enemies. It is both symbolic and ironic that he is able to use his crippled ugliness as a weapon against those who caused it. At the same time that he takes sadistic pleasure in destructiveness, the Laughing Man is able to evoke sympathy and compassion. He rejects the hostile world and forms close, loyal ties of friendship with other misfits. He courageously fights death and evil, but the human world eventually destroys him when it robs him of the purpose of his life.

"The Laughing Man" serial is a harsh, grim reminder of Salinger's view of the hostility in the world. The fact that the narrator, even as an adult, feels close ties of affinity to this grotesque misfit is both tragic and unnerving.

The grotesque tale has great appeal to the boys in the Club. Most of them, one suspects, are victims of adult rejection and hostility, and it is easy to understand their imaginative desires for revenge. To the joy of his boyish admirers, the Laughing Man does what they are unable to do-he gains power over those who try to destroy him. He becomes the ultimate ideal of both rebellion and heroic loyalty.

Parallel Story

Outside the world of fantasy, the boys have another ideal: John Gedsudski. The implication of the story is that he is a rare adult: gentle, understanding and above all a person whom the boys can trust. They admire and respect him. They do not resent the authority that John has over them, because he does not betray their trust.

Even in the choice of a girl-friend, John demonstrates good judgment, to the narrator's way of thinking. Mary, after being put to the test, turns out to be another genuine, unpretentious adult whom the children admire. Mary is so direct that it is not possible for the boys to resent her; thus, they sympathize with her at the end of the story. By the story's end, the boys have acquired significant experience about the mysterious opposite sex and also about the sometimes troubled relations between the sexes.

"The Laughing Man" installments usually mirror John's emotional state. The ending has a forceful ambiguity, in its mingling of make-believe and real anguish. The boys have been moved by the events of real life through the medium of fantasy.

Spirit Of Childhood

The narrator is perhaps one of Salinler's most appealing portraits of a child. He is a mixture of rowdiness, selfishness, intense interest and participation, loyalty and generosity. Surely the confusions, the drives, the spirit of a child's imagination have been depicted as well here as in any other work of literature. The narrator is thus, symbolically, every young boy, and he is highly appealing and amusing. Perhaps his greatest appeal lies in the fact that he still has the capacity to enjoy life and to commit himself to relationships with people, without the utterly doomed assurance that the world will destroy him. He and the other boys felt an affinity for the Laughing Man because he was successfully rebellious against evil, not because he was fated to be a misfit. One is left with the impression, however, that by the time he has grown up, the narrator identifies himself as a misfit among hostile people, with little chance of success at living a happy life. The nine-year-old narrator still has a capacity for joy.

"DOWN AT THE DINGHY"

Child's World Of Retreat

One interpretation of this story is that of a mother's patient penetration of a child's world of retreat and escape from confusion and puzzling and painful snubs. Boo Boo is seen as a mother of rare imagination and compassion, whose posture toward her environment seems faintly amused and ironic, but appreciative, not out of touch. Thus she seems able to establish a direct line of communication with her son Lionel, and ultimately coaxes him back into that world which has troubled him. She restores confidence and joy.

Another interpretation of this story is that there is an unnatural relationship between the mother and the son. And the child's retreat from the world is a retreat from a relationship which he does not understand and feels ambivalent toward.

The Portrait Of A Mother

Boo Boo Tannenbaum (one of the Glass girls before her marriage, as we find out in *Franny and Zooey*) at first seems rather average. The reader is prepared to like her. She seems to have an almost instinctive knowledge of how to deal with her child's retreat.

Like Seymour in the first story in this collection, Boo Boo is one of those rare adults in Salinger's world who are able to keep open the lines of communication to the mind of a child. Everything Boo Boo does seems to be right. Her own ego seems to be secure, seldom in jeopardy. She therefore is confident enough (even though there may be some guilt involved in her relationship with the boy) so that she need not intimidate the way many adults do-whether with other adults or with children.

The Dialogue

The heart of this story (and "heart" may be taken both literally and figuratively) is Boo Boo's dialogue with her son. She relies on her knowledge of what a child values: imaginative secrets and ruthless fair play. Boo Boo is clever enough to appeal to Lionel's sense of justice and to distract the child from his worries with a fantasy secret. She seems to arm the boy with a confidence that enables him to return to a real world. But the reader wonders whether it is a false security that will crumble when he has to face his inner conflicts again.

Comfort Given

When Lionel gives his reason for running away, Boo Boo comforts him, thus winning him over with a mother's love. The reader realizes his pain has been very acute, and he is longing for comfort and understanding from someone who loves him.

Literary Technique

The detailed, mysterious description of Sandra and Mrs. Snell dramatically involves the reader in the mystery of Lionel's problem.

This story demonstrates particularly well Salinger's perceptive use of descriptive details which make people, places and things unforgettable. For example, the description of Mrs. Snell is interesting, humorous and slightly eccentric. The reader is led to wonder about her and the other characters. And typical of Salinger, the questions he raises are not quite answered, although the intrigue is increased. (Salinger's devices here are suggestive of the popular spy story, epitomized by Ian Fleming, where the reader's interest is sustained by the appeal of curious and slightly eccentric descriptions.)

Symbolism

The dinghy is an effective symbol for a child's escape world. It is separate from the dock (i.e., the hostile world) and yet still tied to it. Lionel refuses to let an adult into his private world, until a reconciliation takes place. While isolated in the dinghy, Lionel is a typical Salinger child-protagonist: solitary, solemn, secretive and sensitive.

"FOR ESME-WITH LOVE AND SQUALOR"

This story portrays the "squalor" or "phoniness" which Salinger sees as part of a confusing world made of that "squalor" and, in part, of "niceness." In French's terms, this story expresses "the depressive extreme of Salinger's vision" which swings between "the manic and depressive."

The Unforgettable Esme

Esme is one of Salinger's most unforgettable characters. She is memorable because of her speech, distinguished by repetitions of certain words and most of all by startling but quaint and tender malapropisms (wrong usage of words). In addition, she has a fairly large although slightly eccentric vocabulary, and she talks rather incessantly. She has a forlorn eagerness to understand to know and to analyze things.

Esme combines the sincerity, cool toughness and compassion that Salinger often uses in portraying sensitive, intelligent young people. And yet, Esme seems very real, possibly because she is individualized by distinctive character and personal traits. She further emerges as capable and responsible, perhaps beyond her 13 years.

The strangest thing about Esme is that she is able to discuss all of her painful wartime experiences in a detached manner, almost too detached and self-controlled, in fact. There is a strange quality in her endless chatter in which she does not appear to be emotionally involved.

Sergeant X

Sergeant X's emotional instability and character are drawn by vague suggestions. There is a suggestion at the beginning that he is impulsive. He is described as a loner whose behavior is antisocial. He seems alienated from his fellow soldiers. Nevertheless, he engages freely in conversation with Esme and delights her small brother. The children relax him and he is moved emotionally by the experience of meeting them. Sergeant X is likeable and inspires the reader's interest and sympathy.

Squalor

Esme's interest in squalor is stated, but never explored by Salinger. The reader suspects that she is too genuine and charming, despite her wartime experiences, to have any real knowledge of what she is requesting. She seems to chatter about squalor in the same detached, light manner that she discusses choir practice. One suspects that her healing influence upon the narrator (Sergeant X) is caused, in part, by the fact that the girl who is so interested in squalor is totally untouched by it. She is completely innocent of its meaning. Her purity, her open, warm friendship and her poise are in sharp contrast to Sergeant X's emotional state. (Squalor and phoniness are synonymous in Salinger's work.)

Esme's Influence

In the latter part of the story the sergeant is physically and emotionally ill. His suffering has stripped him of the desire or ability to cope with life.

Esme's simple, warm letter destroys the sergeant's feeling of hopelessness. Her concern is genuine; she is able to reach the man and releases his taut nerves, relaxing him. Sergeant X, we take it, will now be able to feel again, to love again. Note, in the interest of unity, the reference to Dostoevski's recollected words about hell being the inability to love; and to the two spelled-out words in the story, one relating to the narrator and the other to her father, linking them, suggesting that the narrator has been saved from a spiritual or emotional death by Esme's spontaneous offer.

Childhood Innocence

In this story, Salinger seems to stretch his obsessive affection for children a little too far. It is difficult to imagine that a child's innocent concern could replace the need for mental therapy. Nevertheless, Esme's lighthearted letter is an effective device to suggest the disparity between real squalor and real innocence. Esme's self-control (i.e., her lack of self-pity, presumably the result of an autocratic heritage and training) has a powerful influence on Sergeant X. Innocence triumphs over squalor.

"PRETTY MOUTH AND GREEN MY EYES"

A "triangle" with a twist and a shock ending, this story seems to be a slightly vicious-surely a cynical-exercise in unpredictable human psychology. Quite dramatic, a combination of descriptive detail and dialogue, the story relies heavily for its effects on a fairly grotesque situation and on sustaining a good deal of suspense.

Suspense And Surprise

From the first line of the story, there is no way of knowing what is happening, although the reader is aroused to interest and begins to unravel the truth during the long dialogue between Arthur and Lee. It is obvious, though, from the first paragraph, that the two on the sofa are lovers.

There are actually two surprises in the ending. First, there is Arthur's pathetic second call in which he tries to restore his pride and self-respect. The second surprise is less startling perhaps, but is what amounts to justification for all the information gleaned during the story about the troubled existence of Arthur and Joanie. The reader learns a great deal about the three characters, but as usual the author places responsibility outside his story for concluding what these people are really like.

Twentieth-Century Neurosis

According to Salinger's view, Lee, Arthur and Joanie represent a cross-section of twentieth-century American urban society, particularly in a metropolis such as New York. They are moderately affluent, professionally ambitious, often personally confused and neurotic.

Arthur certainly emerges as severely neurotic and insecure and a bit paranoiac. He seems near hysteria as both his marriage and career approach collapse. He has very ambivalent feelings toward Joanie, which combine possessiveness and resentment. Arthur is desperate and tries to save face pathetically. He thinks he is faking composure to Lee, but the **irony** of the situation makes Arthur's plight seem even more pathetic.

Joanie, too, seems insecure, needing attention and reassurance which her husband has not been able to give her. At the same time, however, her remarks to Lee express a callous disregard for her husband.

Lee, for the most part, is quiet and cool, but at the same time he is sensitive to Arthur's desperation as the younger man's panic increases. The final lines of the story indicate Lee's own personal turmoil, which the reader believes includes a mixture of guilt and compassion, a compassion Joanie is probably incapable of. The reader senses that the "triangle" will be changed in the future.

"DE DAUMIER-SMITH'S BLUE PERIOD"

A flashback opens this sprawling story; it seems to attempt to make several points: (1) Life is phony and at times utterly grotesque; (2) Joy seems to be an emotion that can be captured only here and there, momentarily: (3) Everyone is essentially isolated. (The device of the flashback is not as effective as in "Esme" - where the evocation of the present is an indication of the narrator's present state of affairs, his rebirth which we see at the story's end.)

The Narrator

The young man is a typical Salinger **protagonist**: nervously artistic, compulsively involved in conflict with the crasser elements of the external world, introverted and secretive, antisocial and happiest when in retreat into a fantasy world.

The Phony And The Grotesque

There are several indications that the narrator has had a growing conviction of the phoniness of the world. In an engagingly adolescent way, he too becomes a phony, but a refreshingly humorous phony, at that. In the samples of commercial art that he submits to the art school, he is satirically aware of the lack of sincerity in that medium. Given such a disenchanted view of commercial America, one wonders if the narrator does not sense at the outset that the Yoshotos are also phony.

De Daumier-Smith is surrounded by hypocrites and phonies, particularly some of his art students whom Salinger presents in a hilarious piece of satirical writing. Only the nun seems to represent someone who is genuine. The young man, in a singularly funny, fumbling, somewhat pathetic manner, attempts to establish communication and fellowship with her, because he imagines her as his soulmate.

The events in Canada are so satirically comic that they approach the grotesque. The absurdities accumulate as the story progresses. The idea of the grotesque is epitomized in the orthopedic appliance shop where both of the narrator's "epiphanies" occur, the second suggesting vaguely that the young man has a moment of mystic insight.

Alienation

The hero feels alienated both in New York and in Canada. In New York, he becomes progressively alienated from the city's hustle and bustle and from his stepfather. In Canada, he seems to arrive at the conclusion that withdrawal is one solution to the grotesque and the phony life: everybody, it is implied, is of necessity isolated (or at any rate, rate sensitive and imaginative are forced by the rest of the world into a nunlike existence).

De Daumier's attraction to the nun is probably also an attraction to her isolation from the world's hostility in a haven safe from hypocrisy. He creates fantasies about a pure relationship with Sister Irma, but even his fantasy is shattered by the harsh world (Father Zimmermann).

Happiness And Joy

For the narrator, complete happiness is elusive, even impossible. He indicates his malevolent view of the world and his chances of finding true happiness there. The best the young man comes to hope for are fleeting moments of joy-especially those times when he can momentarily triumph over a hostile environment. De Daumier's moments of elation are sweet though short-lived. His personal satisfaction surely stems from his momentary refusal to adjust to (and participate in) the hypocrisy of the world, as represented by the completely phony art school.

Cynical Tolerance

We note, however, that after the narrator's experience at the appliance shop in the blinding, rising sun, he calmly writes letters to his four expelled students. This gesture suggests a cynical tolerance of the phony world, with one important difference-he is more "his own man" than at the beginning of his Canadian experience. He recognizes better his own capacities for joy, however fleeting, and his ability to exercise control over the external world.

The reader realizes that the young man is just as repelled by his own insincerity as by that in the external world. There is a suggestion that he will fake reality less in the future himself, now that he has a glimpse of the meaning and consequences of phoniness.

"TEDDY"

This famous story, considered by some to be marred by its perverse, ambiguous ending, constantly raises questions which maintain the reader's interest without descending to slick suspense. Is Teddy a genuine prodigy and genius, simply precocious and self-conscious, or in fact a nasty, spoiled brat? Does Teddy represent the ultimate example (morbid, though it is) of Salinger's "salvation-by-child" themes, since Teddy's theories of education, his sturdy individuality and his brand of mysticism seem to have the author's approval? In addition to a curiously aged little boy, the story is graced by some of Salinger's most credible detail, both with respect to the setting on board a ship at sea and to the other characters.

Eastern Mysticism

Salinger's philosophical and mystic preoccupations (which practically overshadow considerations of literary craftsmanship by the time we get to "Zooey") are suggested in "Teddy." In fact, "Teddy" seems like Salinger's testing ground for *Franny and Zooey* which several years later developed more fully a synthesis between Eastern and Western thought. In both stories, the mystical ideas are clearly drawn from Zen Buddhism. Zen Buddhism is a Buddhist sect in Japan, originated in India.

The aim of Zen Buddhism is enlightenment, or realization of one's inner self; it is achieved primarily by meditation (one of Teddy's preoccupations). Buddhism is also suggested in Teddy's theories of pantheism (doctrine that God is everything and everything is God); denial of a permanent self in the doctrine of reincarnation; and the destruction of the principles of logic, particularly the Law of Identity (principle that a thing is what it is; that is, everything in the universe has finite dimensions). In addition, there is a direct suggestion of the Platonic doctrine of innate ideas (that one has certain knowledge at birth).

The Enigmatic Teddy

Teddy seems to be a kind of Salinger ideal - the really adult child. He is quietly individual, politely holding his own with adults when he must, but usually handling them in a humane manner. He resists coercion from adults or other liberties which they may try to take (such as condescension). He can put an adult in his place without being obnoxious.

There is no indication that Teddy is a misfit or the neurotic, manic-depressive type often found in Salinger's stories. In fact, he is the opposite, because of his awareness of the external world and his desire to observe conventionalities. Teddy is rather detached from the ordinary world, but wishes to go along with it.

The young hero is both a rationalist (believes that truth and knowledge are discernible by the mind without reference to sense perceptions) and a humanist (interested in human interests and values), but he avoids sentimentality and excessive emotionality. His own enlightenment is claimed in behalf of the theory of reincarnation, but Teddy's theory of educating children could be applied without the sanction of Eastern philosophical mysticism.

Teddy is regarded by some critics as a "cold fish," because of his views on emotions. He makes a distinction between the true depth of feeling (which, for him, stems from an impersonal, detached regard for others) and slobbering sentimentality. As a rationalist he is opposed to emotionality. Nevertheless, he loves God and his parents according to his own definition.

The Ending: A Mistake

From Teddy's belief in reincarnation and his casual attitude toward death, from his mystical ability to sense when death will occur, from his anticipation of his own death-from all these hints the reader might be prepared for the death of Teddy at the end. Readers and critics are usually in almost angry disagreement, however, as to what has happened at the story's end. The reader wants to believe, one suspects that Teddy has been killed, an ending logically prepared for. Yet if things have been enacted the way Teddy envisioned, why would the malicious Booper scream? Also, we can make a good case for the female scream to be reverberating from out of the cavern of an empty pool. In addition, considering Salinger's view of logic presented in the story, there is some reason to suspect that he would not choose a totally logical ending. It is a fair criticism of this tight, challenging tale that Salinger has overstepped suspense in the ending, into a perverse, even precious ambiguity

Teddy's Family

The dominant motif in the relationship among the members of the McArdle family in that of hostility. Booper is dominated by sadistic impulses. She is cruel to Myron, hostile toward the world in general, and she express general hatred, particularly toward Teddy.

The parent's hostility toward one another is particularly outspoken and harsh. In a sense, the general hostility in Teddy's environment provides ample reason for him to withdraw into meditation and be casual toward the idea of leaving this life. It offers him little in the way of genuine warmth. His mother's sentimental pampering is more of a release for her own emotional needs than a response to a son she really understands. Teddy's parents could not possibly communicate with him on his own level. He is totally isolated, intellectually and spiritually. He is able to communicate somewhat with Bob Nicholson, but Nicholson does not really understand Teddy, though he tries.

World Of Lost Childhood

There are suggestions that Teddy may be attracted to Oriental philosophy precisely because it negates the use of the mind (reason), which had distinguished him from other people (particularly other children), in favor of the pure and primary world of childhood sensation. This, then, would be the world of lost childhood that Salinger always weaves into his work. It is a pre-Edenite world of bliss where knowledge is the serpent of evil, because it is a false and precocious show of knowledge, which isolates and alienates children from their environment without emancipating these innocent victims and teaching them how to cope with life and to communicate with others.

FRANNY AND ZOOEY

"FRANNY"

Setting Forth The Struggles Of A "Pilgrim"

Although the reader is introduced in the first pages to Lane Coutell, the real subject under scrutiny throughout this section of the novel is Franny herself-Franny looking deeply at herself and finding out about herself, her relationships to people and her place in the world. The answers to her questions emerge more clearly in the second, longer "Zooey" portion of the novel. Franny is one of Salinger's hypersensitized, searching people (and something of a misfit like Zooey, we see later). Her responses to Lane illuminate her current struggle to be honest with herself and others, yet become at peace with herself in relation to the rest of the world. As suggested by the small book which has had enormous influence upon her, her quest is at present that of a pilgrim.

The Themes Of Phoniness, Niceness And Integrity

In a sense *Franny and Zooey* is a more mature work than either *The Catcher in the Rye* or *Nine Stories* in that Salinger has brought together in one character's struggle for self-honesty (or two-Franny and Zooey) questions about what is phony and what is "nice." Or, in other words, the resolution of the conflict about how to be oneself (how to retain personal integrity), yet remain in some kind of realistic, meaningful contact with the rest of the world. This struggle is placed within the character-internalized, shall we say. Franny, in short, as we see even more clearly in the "Zooey" **episode**, is attempting to define herself and take responsibility for her selfhood in the midst of a very important sorting out of various elements of her "socialization" thus far: acquisition of knowledge, with or without wisdom; relating to another person; choosing what to do with one's life.

All of these elements of socialization are reminiscent of *The Catcher in the Rye*-they are a more mature, college version of Holden Caulfield's adolescent quest for truth and identity. Franny is acutely and self-consciously aware of the disparity between her values (in literature, education, religion and life) and the values of those around her. There are her college acquaintances (like Lane) who are somewhat pompous pseudo-intellectuals pursuing a conventional, upper-middle-class set of values as though engaged in a mindless ritual. There are her teachers who seem intent upon destroying literary values and intimidating students with a shallow show of brilliance. Franny cannot cope with or adjust to the pettiness in the world around her.

Confused and worried by her struggle to find out what her own values are, Franny feels guilty at the same time. She hates the destructiveness of others, but feels that she, too, is destructive, if only in her own thoughts. She feels out of touch with Lane and other people, because what they do and say really does not interest her. She feels that somehow perhaps it should. She finds herself attacking Lane's values, implying that they are stupid or inconsequential. On the other hand, she pretends to be interested in their conversation and thus fakes the reality of the situation by being dishonest. She suffers additional guilt-she has betrayed both Lane's and her own values, in order to be nice. Tension mounts as Franny's guilt and confusion mount.

Franny is tormented because she cannot bear to live by everyone else's values (as she has been doing on the surface), and yet she cannot find genuine first-hand values of her own. She attributes the shallow dishonesty of others to their obsession with self (ego) - their desire to make a flamboyant display or to be a success. Afraid that she will be drawn toward these values also, she withdraws from people and their pursuits, thus hoping to retain some measure of integrity to her own values, confused as they are. She hopes to find solace in the destruction of her ego.

Alienation And Vulnerability

As the security of Lane and Franny, as a couple, becomes more and more threatened, they withdraw into their separate and somewhat hostile worlds. The barriers between them become more and more impassable. Each of them in his own separate self-consciousness is trying to shift the responsibility for discontent and insecurity onto the other. Franny is detached, it seems, almost in spite of herself. She seems to be yearning for a relationship that is genuine and to which she can fully commit herself without fear of the vulnerability that such a commitment implies. Her tragedy is that she can find no one whom she respects enough to really care about. Lane, on the other hand, would be incapable of such a commitment or of being vulnerable. His defenses are intended as a protection against real or anticipated pain - the pain that is always a possibility when two people let themselves be close enough in a relationship to be hurt by it.

The unfortunate **irony**, Salinger seems to say, is that socialization prevents two people from communicating honestly and affecting that very peace with self that Franny is seeking. That is, socialization often obscures the more honest response. Franny becomes more hostile as she tries harder not to be hostile. This results in Lane's further withdrawal and defensive attitude toward her. Their mutual alienation is at once tragic and infuriating. Lane is completely insensitive, Franny is too sensitive, almost out of touch with reality. Neither one of them has an understanding of why the alienation exists. Both seem to be fundamentally lonely.

Reality

In fact, the reader wonders where true reality lies. Are either Lane or Franny in touch with it? Is reality a matter of football weekends and shallow values, or is it some kind of rarefied mystical experience? One senses that the real tragedy of the novel (and of many people's lives) is that neither Lane nor Franny is in control of or in touch with true reality. Both have chosen false alternatives. There is a tremendous gap between Lane's "practical" world and Franny's impractical solution to its crassness and lack of meaning. Like many well-intentioned do-gooders, Franny seems just as out of touch with life as Lane, who lacks wisdom and sensitivity.

Franny's Idealization Of Beauty

Franny is desperately searching for both a moral and an aesthetic ideal. She expresses her literary ideal of poetic beauty rather inarticulately. Her inarticulateness makes the reader aware that she is struggling for a concept which she does not fully understand yet. Franny's ideal of literary beauty centers around literature which has depth and universal, profound meaning to people. She is repulsed by the shallow literature produced by so many writers - a literature which is pretentiously clever and studied and overly self-conscious. Yet she is unable to communicate clearly what she means by the concept "beautiful."

Quest For A Moral Ideal

Franny's search for a moral ideal has led her to a treasured little book, *The Way of a Pilgrim*. She attempts to communicate to Lane the meaning of this book to her, but she is afraid also, aware that he is too insensitive to even understand that she should bother to concern herself about moral ideals. The little book suggests a means by which a person can communicate with God and have this communication reach into the center of his being, thus bringing insight.

To the reader, however, the pilgrim emerges as more of a sentimentalized, impractical portrait than Franny can yet perceive. The pilgrim's search, and thus Franny's search for insight through the Jesus Prayer, are genuine, but they are too remote and romanticized. A pilgrim should not intellectualize and withdraw from other people. Insight is not to be automatically gained by repeatedly murmuring a prayer. Franny has yet to learn this. At this point, she is swept off her feet by an idyllic tale of a wanderer who is serving humanity in what Franny believes to be a truly noble way-his sole mission is to help others to find the insight he has gained. To Franny - a sensitive, confused, romantic girl - the pilgrim's noble purpose seems so much purer than the material concerns of daily life. The pilgrim has profound religious values which seem, to Franny at least, to

BRIGHT NOTES STUDY GUIDE

be so far superior to the petty shallowness which engulfs her in every pursuit and in every relationship she encounters.

Letters Used To Reveal Characters

It is interesting that in both the "Franny" and the "Zooey" sections of the novel, letters are utilized to reveal characters who are not present (Franny, Buddy) and to suggest the writer's powerful influence upon the recipient. This approach is, of course, a very legitimate literary device. Thus, in Franny's letter to Lane we get not only a sense of her spontaneity (indeed, her tendency to manic moods) but an idea of how she thinks of Lane, her current conflict about knowledge, education and poetry, and her degree of socialization.

"ZOOEY"

Psychology Of Characters Revealed Through Inaction

Similar to *The Catcher in the Rye*, this novel is a novel of internal conflicts and responses. Very little action takes place, particularly in the "Zooey" section. The main interest and "action" are psychological.

Despite the minimum of physical action, we learn a great deal about the Glass family, as well as about the particular psyches and problems of Franny and Zooey. The precociousness, eccentricity and intensity of the whole family are illustrated through facts revealed in Zooey's thoughts and conversations (particularly with Mrs. Glass) and in Buddy's letter. In addition, Salinger provides biographical information in a footnote. (As an aesthetic device, footnotes are a subject of dispute. At best, many claim, they are a jarring disruption of a fictional narrative; their proper place is in a work of nonfiction. Salinger acknowledges this view in the footnote himself.)

Zooey undergoes a personal self-analysis which prepares him for his lecture to Franny, which culminates in the resolution of Franny's emotional and spiritual crisis and her discovery of peace of mind.

In the midst of all this, of course, a good many customary Salinger **themes** are treated: Zen Buddhism, his theories of education, the nature of illusory differences between things, alienation and the problem of communication with other human beings.

Significance Of Buddy's Letter

First of all, the letter is a literary device to fill us in on Zooey's considerable, but eccentric background of knowledge and his current career. Zooey's decision to reread the letter indicates his own need for self-definition. It is a symptom of some inner questioning and discontent. He rereads it in search of some assistance in the face of the career decision that he must soon make. The influence of Zen Buddhism and related theories of knowledge is indicated in the letter.

There is also Buddy's hint at the meaning of truth: truth can only be arrived at when the illusory differences between things or between people (that are often improperly categorized or labelled) are destroyed. Thus, boys and girls, life and death, grief and delight, etc., share much in common. Both Franny and Zooey have a similar problem, in Salinger's view. They have strong likes and dislikes; they are too concerned with finite dimensions and individuality (ego) to be able to gain true knowledge-knowledge requiring the renunciation of both the ego and concepts of finiteness.

Early Childhood Influences

When examined more thoroughly, the seemingly humorous vein in which the Glass children are described opens onto a more pathetic picture of youngsters being cheated of childhood and being possibly thrust into precocious and artificial postures which come back to haunt their adult development. The title of the quiz program is ironic, for these children (especially) may be held back from true wisdom. Their precocious intellectuality does not guarantee that they will have great insight or a true awareness and sensitivity to reality or to other people.

We see this dilemma in Franny's questionings about the relation between knowledge and wisdom, as well as in Seymour's concept of knowledge. Franny finds that the world is crucially lacking in wisdom, even though men of intelligence do exist. The reader may recall that this was a dominant **theme** in *The Catcher in the Rye*.

Zooey seems very self-consciously aware that he and Franny are alienated from other people and from a true knowledge of reality and other people. Neither can adjust to or cope with the situation. Zooey tries to rationalize his own sense of isolation by transferring responsibility, but without really convincing himself.

Mrs. Glass, in a pathetically inarticulate, emotional way, senses that her children have changed greatly since childhood. They have lost the happiness of youth, a happiness she misses and is helpless to help her children regain. She is totally alienated from them and is unaware of the meaning of Franny's and Zooey's spiritual struggles and conflict. She has neither the intellectual ability nor the sensitivity to help her youngest two children find the insight they so desperately are searching for.

Salinger's Insight Into The Human Condition - A Humorous Instance

One of the joys of reading Salinger (unless to excess) is his whimsical insight into human beings (in excess, it may be regarded as a studied cleverness). Salinger is aware of how people like to be "in" on the secrets of other human beings. Instead of being regarded as an example of dead-end naturalistic detail, the cataloging of the contents of the medicine cabinet may be taken as representative of at least one repository of family intimacies and secrets.

Insight - A Serious Instance

It seems very important to Salinger that he make a point about the close proximity in the human psyche and emotional setup between grief and delight, no doubt suggesting that the human condition is that these two can and perhaps must follow one upon the other. Buddy's recollection of the airplane incident is a bit like the story-within-the-story in "The Laughing Man," which also focuses upon the "grotesque" which exists in the midst of real human grief. This is also an emphasis on the incredible, even absurd fact of aliveness in the midst of death, a fact that inevitably requires a reassertion of the life principle. Buddy's description of the doll on the plane suggests this theme.

Alienation

The alienation **theme** is reasserted in the "Zooey" section of the novel. It is explored at length in Mrs. Glass's conversation with Zooey. They are pathetically unable to communicate; the shower curtain is a symbolic barrier between mother and son. Zooey is hostile to Bessie's cliches, her prying and her childish misunderstanding of Franny's breakdown. Bessie's insight into her children's problems may be oversimplified, but she is at least able to identify Zooey's difficulties in relationships with people.

The alienation between brother and sister is suggested in Franny and Zooey's conversation by the fact that Franny cannot see him while he is talking to her. In addition, coldness and isolation are suggested by the paperweight. Throughout this section, there are images of snowflakes, blizzards and ice that are sharply contrasted to the scene of emotional warmth and joy that Zooey sees out the window. The final posture of alienation is Franny's face-down position on the couch.

The **irony**, of course, is that the moment when Zooey and Franny are least alienated from one another-on the phone-is the moment when they are totally separated. Zooey, at this moment, is just a voice across a wire, but they are able at least to communicate warmly for the first time.

The End Of The Pilgrimage

The most crucial scene in the novel is Zooey's discussion with Franny. He makes ruthlessly clear to Franny that she is unrealistic and that there can be no withdrawal from the world (or from duty) into a safe haven of inaction. In this scene, Franny and Zooey provide each other with insight which allows Franny her first peace of mind.

The implication of their discussion is that Franny not only does not see Jesus for what He is (she idealizes or alters Him to suit her own vision of religious truth), but she also does not see people as they really are. Franny, the **theme** of this section states, must learn to face reality maturely-a reality not of idealized people, but of both good and evil people. She must learn to acknowledge and to deal with both.

To be able to live realistically, Salinger suggests, Franny must develop a Christian vision which applies to this earth, not to a romanticized, adolescent world of plaster saints. She must learn that true Christianity exists right under her nose and can be practiced in everyday life; it does not require a pilgrimage or crusade to save souls all over the earth. The souls are everywhere; they are symbolized by Seymour's Fat Lady, a symbol for the divine spirit in everyone who lives. Franny's truth lies here-in the "religious" world of the mundane concerns of everyday life, to which she must fully commit herself.

Franny's pilgrimage ends when Zooey convinces here that her own patronizing, superior attitude is a pompous means of escaping Christian truth and true Christian duty. Franny's Jesus Prayer can have no meaning as long as it has no content and she tries to escape from reality into a fantasy world of pilgrims and religious seers. She has to learn to take meaningful religious action, not just spend her time reciting prayers incessantly. Zooey's phone conversation finally makes Franny aware of her mistake and of the real meaning of Seymour's and Buddy's religious views. Her internal conflict is finally resolved.

Synthesis Of Eastern And Western Philosophy

Franny's quest is clearly a quest for an understanding of the principles of Zen Buddhism (see discussion of "Teddy" in *Nine Stories* below). The incessant prayer serves the same purpose as Buddhist meditation-by fixing one's attention on one thing, one's mind passes through stages of absorption or self-hypnosis to a true enlightenment. Blended with this idea of meditation is a Christian morality of self-sacrifice. The synthesis amounts to total ego renunciation and destruction of the Western notion of individuality.

The Glass children all seem to suffer from having a great store of knowledge, by a knowledge that does not help them to live happy lives, to cope with the hostility of the world, or to establish strong ties of communication to other people. Salinger's answer to this problem seems to be that people must either remain alienated (as Salinger seems to alienate himself) or they must lose their personal individuality by renouncing the ego and any attempt at self-knowledge.

CHARACTER ANALYSES

Lane Coutell

He seems to be a mixture of individualist and fairly socialized traits. He is obviously socially at ease enough to arrange in some manner for Franny's college weekend with him. He is absentminded in a typical Salinger way and is something of a sentimentalist or at least a romantic. We are told respectively that Lane is brilliant, nice, phony, concerned about Franny and self-centered-all of these qualities are probably present.

Franny Glass

Like so many of Salinger's protagonists, Franny is a sensitive young searcher, caught in the moment of this novel (for she is also a Phoebe Caulfield or a Boo Boo Tannenbaum) at a point of crisis between what seems phony and nice, hypocritical and real in herself and the world. The circumstances here find her searching among her elements: college, the theatre, a boyfriend, beloved brothers and an eccentric but closeknit family structure. Franny is attempting a just transition from the child's world of dolls and saints into an adult world of responsibility and maturer joys. And we see that the special elements in her background work both for and against her ultimate experience of truth or insight.

Zooey Glass

At twenty-five, Zooey seems established in the professional direction he is pursuing, but with doubts and questions. For the message he passes on to Franny at the end of the novel is for himself also: whatever you choose to do, do it wholeheartedly, as a fully alive person. A commitment is a commitment and requires your responsible participation. Zooey too, in other words, has been both assisted and restrained by the similar and eccentric influences of the Glass family upon his life. It can be claimed that Zooey also grows, resolves himself, during the novel.

Mrs. Glass

She is vividly and interestingly depicted, and evokes our sympathy. Undoubtedly eccentric, she is just as obviously loved by her children, even though she exasperates them at times. She has occasional and profound insights which are very paradoxical.

Note

It is worth noting that the Glass family as sketched in the first pages of "Zooey" (particularly in the author's footnote) has its appearance directly or indirectly in *Nine Stories*. Older sister Boo Boo is the Boo Boo Tannenbaum of "Down at the Dinghy"; Walt is the lighthearted soldier, Eloise's first boy-friend, in "Uncle Wiggily in Connecticut"; Zooey of the "authentic esprit" is the precocious and partly lovable Teddy of "Teddy." Mrs. Glass and Seymour, of course, are seen in "A Perfect Day for Bananafish."

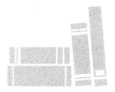

FRANNY AND ZOOEY

. . . .

Question: What is the meaning of "The Way of a Pilgrim" in the book?

Answer: This is the title of the book which Franny is carrying in her pocketbook. It emerges in conversation latter as a mystical treatise which has had profound impact on her thinking, or more accurately, her current re-evaluation of her life, her activities, her philosophies. Actually, it is a part of her heritage from Seymour, her oldest brother, and indirectly from the next oldest brother, Buddy. Basically, the book sets forth principles embodied in a "Jesus Prayer," which when said long enough brings about the true knowledge of God, a response from God; this is also consistent with Eastern philosophy (i.e., Zen Buddhism), and all of this religious background has been passed down to her from Seymour and Buddy, but at this particular moment in her life seems to be bearing fruit, part of it bitter fruit. In a larger sense, though, the entire novel *Franny and Zooey* is about Franny's (and to some extent Zooey's) pilgrimage, since the end brings about insight or truth for her, the "response" she has been seeking and has suffered toward.

BRIGHT NOTES STUDY GUIDE

Question: Discuss the implications of "It's A Wise Child."

Answer: All of the Glass children appeared at some point in the time span of sixteen years on a radio quiz program by this title, and they became rather well known. The fact of this participation in a successful quiz program pinpoints their intelligence, of course, but also their background of showmanship, overdramatization, and overintellectualization. The ironic point is, of course, that a smart-as-a-whip child is by no means a wise child, and indeed the terms may be mutually exclusive. For all the Glass children have had to struggle toward wisdom out of their experience and their so-called knowledge. For one thing, many of the elements in their childhood have isolated, even alienated them from other people, and later in life each one of them has had to re-evaluate and re-orient himself to the outside world.

Question: How do we know that the question of self-honesty bothers Franny?

Answer: In the first section, Franny is most concerned with what is going on in her consciousness in relation to Lane, because she finds herself estranged from him, easily irritated by him, in the light of the private upheavals she has been feeling. We have as example the several instances where she acknowledges to herself guilt feelings right after having concealed a more honest, negative response toward him. Franny is also bothered by the fact that she has, up till now, been willing to live by the standards and values of other people. She is terrified that she will continue to do so. She wants to have integrity more than any other virtue. Phoniness repels her, especially whatever phoniness she sees in herself. In the second half of the book, of course, Franny moves, painfully and through the assistance of Zooey, to the resolution of the problem of personal integrity.

Question: What would you say is, briefly summarized, the implication of the ending?

Answer: Basically, it is the revelation of "God-in-us," through rather typical Salinger devices. Stated another way, it goes back to the idea that the true Christian spirit attempts to get rid of illusory differences which separate and alienate people. Part of the "message" is to stress the likeness of human beings, in short their "godness." An awareness of this "godness" is the only thing that makes it possible for men to live in the spirit of love, according to Salinger. Franny's pilgrimage comes to an end at the moment that she understands the Christ-is-everywhere principle.

BIBLIOGRAPHY AND GUIDE TO FURTHER RESEARCH

. . . .

Aldridge, John L. "The Society of Three Novels," in *In Search of Heresy.* 1956, New York. Says reader of *The Catcher in the Rye* identifies with the **protagonist** but gains no insights; there is pathos without tragedy.

Belcher, William F. and James W. Lee, editors. *J. D. Salinger and the Critics.* 1962, Belmont paperback.

Bowen, Robert O. "The Salinger Syndrome: Charity against Whom?" *Ramparts,* I (May, 1962), 52-60.

Branch, Edgar. "Mark Twain and J. D. Salinger: A Study in Literary Continuity," *American Quarterly,* IX (Summer, 1957), 144-58.

Breit, Harvey. "Reader's Choice," *Atlantic,* CLXXXVIII (August, 1951), 82.

Carpenter, Frederic I. "Adolescent in American Fiction," *English Journal,* XLVI (September, 1957), 313-19.

Corbett, Edward P. J. "Raise High the Barriers, Censors," *America* (November 19, 1960), 441-43.

Costello, Donald P. "The Language of *The Catcher in the Rye,*" *American Speech,* XXXIV (October, 1959), 172-81.

Davis, Tom. "J. D. Salinger: 'Some Crazy Cliff' Indeed," *Western Humanities Review,* XIV (Winter, 1960), 97-99. Catcher related to doctrines of Mahayana Buddhism, in which Salinger has shown interest.

Fiedler, Leslie. "The Eye of Innocence," in *No! In Thunder.* 1960, Boston. See also *Love and Death in the American Novel,* 1960, New York, discussion of Salinger and Jack Kerouac.

French, Warren. *J. D. Salinger* (Twayne Authors). 1963, New York. A comprehensive, scholarly yet interesting study.

Geismar, Maxwell. "J. D. Salinger: The Wise Child and the New Yorker School of Fiction," in *American Moderns: From Rebellion to Conformity.* 1958, New York.

Green, Martin. "Amis and Salinger: The Latitude of Private Conscience," *Chicago Review,* II (Winter, 1958), 20-25.

Gwynn, Frederick L. and Joseph L. Blotner. *The Fiction of J. D. Salinger.* 1958, Pittsburgh. A "monograph" on Salinger, the first. A brief and useful summary of author's achievements.

Grunwald, Henry Anatole, editor. *Salinger: A Critical and Personal Portrait.* 1962, New York. Interesting collection of about two dozen critical articles along with a lengthy introduction by editor.

Hansford, Martin. "The American Problem of Direct Address," *The Western Review,* XVI (Winter, 1952), 101-14.

Hassan, Ihab H. "Rare Quixotic Gesture: The Fiction of J. D. Salinger," in *Radical Innocence: Studies in the Contemporary Novel.* 1961. Princeton, N.J.

Havemann, Ernest. "The Search for the Mysterious J. D. Salinger," *Life,* Nov. 3, 1961, pp. 129-44. Recounts an unsuccessful visit to Cornish, N.Y., to interview Salinger.

Hermann, John. "J. D. Salinger: Hello Hello Hello," *College English*, XXII (January, 1961), 262-64. Discussion of Esme.

Hicks, Granville. "J. D. Salinger: Search for Wisdom," *Saturday Review*, XLII (July 25, 1959), 13-30.

Jacobs, Robert G. "J. D. Salinger's *The Catcher in the Rye:* Holden Caulfield's 'Goddam Autobiography,'" *Iowa English Yearbook* (Fall, 1959), 9-14.

Jones, Ernest. "Case History of All of Us," *Nation*, CLXXIII (Sept. 1, 1951), 176.

Kaplan, Charles. "Holden and Huck: The Odysseys of Youth," *College English*, XVIII (November, 1956), 76-80.

Kazin, Alfred. "J. D. Salinger: 'Everybody's Favorite,'" *The Atlantic*, CCVIII (August, 1961), 27-31.

Kegel, Charles H. "Incommunicability in Salinger: *The Catcher in the Rye*," *Western Humanities Review*, XI (Spring, 1957), 188-90.

Laser, Marvin, and Norman Fruman, editors. *Studies in J. D. Salinger.* 1963, Los Angeles. Reviews and critical articles, emphasis on Catcher.

Levine, Paul. "J. D. Salinger: The Development of the Misfit Hero," *Twentieth Century Literature*, IV (October, 1958), 92-99.

Longstreth, T. Morris. "Review of *The Catcher in the Rye*," *The Christian Science Monitor* (July 19, 1951), 7.

Marks, Barry A. "Holden in the Rye," *College English*, XXIII (March, 1962), 507.

Marple, Anne. "Salinger's Oasis of Innocence," *New Republic*, CXLV (Sept. 18, 1961), 22-23.

Marsden, Malcolm M., editor. *If You Really Want to Know: A Catcher Casebook.* 1963, New York.

Martin, Dexter. "Holden in the Rye," *College English,* XXIII (March, 1962), 507-08.

McCarthy, Mary. "J. D. Salinger's Closed Circuit," *Harper's Magazine,* CCXXV (October, 1962), 46-47.

Mizener, Arthur. "The Love Song of J. D. Salinger," *Harper's Magazine,* CCXVIII (February, 1959), 83-90.

Salinger, J. D. *The Catcher in the Rye.* 1951, Boston (Bantam edition).

____. *Nine Stories.* 1953, Boston (Signet edition).

____. *Franny and Zooey.* 1961, Boston (Bantam edition).

Seng, Peter J. "The Fallen Idol: The Immature World of Holden Caulfield," *College English,* XXIII (December, 1961), 203-09.

Steiner, George. "The Salinger Industry," *Nation* (November 14, 1959), 360-63. His social criticism.

Updike, John. "Anxious Days for the Glass Family," *New York Times Book Review* (Sept. 17, 1961), 1, 52. Reviewed by a contemporary novelist and short story writer.

Wakefield, Dan. "Salinger and the Search for Love," *New World Writing* #14, New York, 1958.

Wells, Arvin R. "Huck Finn and Holden Caulfield: The Situation of the Hero," *The Ohio University Review,* II.

Wiegand, William. "J. D. Salinger: Seventy-Eight Bananas," *Chicago Review,* II (Winter, 1958), 3-19.

Wisconsin Studies in Contemporary Literature, III, No. 3 (Winter, 1963). A valuable Salinger issue.

CPSIA information can be obtained
at www.ICGtesting.com
Printed in the USA
BVHW051207080223
658059BV00017B/689